BLACK WIDOW SPIDERS

THE SPIDER DISCOVERY LIBRARY

Louise Martin

Rourke Enterprises, Inc.
Vero Beach, Florida 32964

LIBRARY OF CONGRESS
Library of Congress Cataloging-in-Publication Data

Martin, Louise, 1955-
  Black widow spiders/by Louise Martin.

  p. cm. — (The Spider discovery library)
  Includes index.
  Summary: Describes the physical characteristics, habits,
and natural environment of the shy but poisonous (female
only) black widow spider.
  ISBN 0-86592-965-3
  1. Black widow spider — Juvenile literature. [1. Black
widow spider. 2. Spiders.] I. Title. II. Series:
Martin, Louise, 1955-
Spider discovery library.
QL458.42.T54M37   1988   88-5966
595.4'4 - dc19   CIP
                             AC

Printed in the USA

*Title page photo: A female black
widow spider climbs a branch*

TABLE OF CONTENTS

BLACK WIDOW SPIDERS

Black widow spiders belong to the *Theridiidae* family of spiders. People used to think that the female black widow spider always ate the male, making herself a widow. This is how the black widow spider got its name. In fact, she does sometimes eat both her mate and her **spiderlings**, but this is quite normal for many female spiders.

A black widow spider on its web

WHERE THEY LIVE

Black widow spiders are found in countries with fairly warm climates. They live in the warmer parts of North America and in Mexico. In Australia, they are called "redbacks," and in New Zealand, they are called "katipos." Black widow spiders also live in the warm countries surrounding the **Mediterranean Sea**. There are four **species** of black widow spiders in the United States.

There are several kinds of black widow spiders

FEMALE BLACK WIDOW SPIDERS

Female black widow spiders are much bigger than the males. Even so, they are quite small. Female black widow spiders grow to about one-half inch long. They have shiny black bodies, and no hair. Young females sometimes have a row of small red spots along their backs. The most common black widow spiders are called *Latrodectus Mactans.* These females have red hourglass-shaped markings on the undersides of their bodies.

The female black widow spider's red markings can be clearly seen

MALE BLACK WIDOW SPIDERS

Male black widow spiders are very small and quite harmless. They are usually less than one-third the size of the females, which makes them only about one-sixth of an inch long. Male black widows also have black, shiny bodies, but do not have any red markings like the females. Unlike the bite of a female, the male black widow spiders' bite is not at all dangerous to humans.

Male black widow spiders are harmless

A female black widow dangles on a thread from her web

A female black widow spider with
her egg sac

HOW THEY GROW

Female black widow spiders live much longer than the males. A female sometimes lives as long as 18 months, but a male's life span is only from 25 to 40 days. Black widow spiders shed their skin in order to grow. This is called **molting**. Female black widows molt seven to nine times before reaching **maturity**. Males only molt between four and seven times.

A black widow wraps its prey in a silk web

BABY BLACK WIDOW SPIDERS

Scientists think that female black widows only have babies once in their lives. They lay their eggs in the early spring, in round **cocoons** about one-half inch across. Each cocoon contains between 250 and 750 eggs. The female spider guards her cocoons very closely. After about thirty days the black widow spiderlings hatch from the eggs.

A black widow spider with its tangled-looking web

PREY

Black widow spiders spin their webs in sheltered places, usually in rock **crevices** or dark corners. The threads are quite fine, but very strong. The web itself is closely woven and tangled-looking. The black widows wait for their **prey** at one side of the web. Whenever the web moves slightly, they rush out to attack. First the spiders bind their prey with silk so that it cannot move, and then inject it with **venom** to **paralyze** it. The prey is then ready to eat.

Female black widow spiders like this are very poisonous

THEIR VENOM

The bite of the female black widow spider is very painful. The poison works fast. Within minutes, the venom causes cramps in the victim's muscles, and he or she finds it difficult to move. Breathing becomes difficult, and the victim develops a high fever and feels faint. Thirty minutes later, the victim is in great pain, but luckily the antitoxin works quickly to relieve the discomfort.

A black widow spider eats a scorpion.

BLACK WIDOW SPIDERS AND PEOPLE

All spiders use poison to kill their prey, but only some spiders' poison is dangerous to humans. The female black widow spider is one of the most poisonous spiders in the world. Her venom is said to be fifteen times more poisonous than that of a rattlesnake. The female black widow's bite can kill a person if the victim does not get treatment. Today there is an **antitoxin** to cure victims.

Glossary

antitoxin (ANT i TOX in) — a drug that fights poisons

cocoon (co COON) — a silk wrap used to protect eggs

crevice (CRE vice) — crack

maturity (mat UR i ty) — adulthood

to molt (MOLT) — to shed an outer layer of skin or hair

Mediterranean Sea (MED i terr A ne an) — a sea between
  Europe and North Africa

paralyze (PAR a lyze) — to make a person or animal unable to move

prey (PREY) — an animal that is hunted for food

species (SPE cies) — a scientific term meaning type or kind

spiderlings (SPI der lings) — baby spiders

venom (VEN om) — poison

INDEX